Flutterbye's Flying Friends

**Written and Illustrated
by
Johnnie W. Lewis**

Marietta, GA USA

In this book, the second in the "Flutterbye, the Butterfly" series, Flutterbye's daughter looks around the area where she lives and learns that there are more creatures that fly than just her! And all of them have the same challenges that she does — what to eat and how NOT to be eaten!

Lewis, Johnnie W.
      flutterbye's flying friends/Johnnie W. Lewis

ISBN 9781495955365
Copyright © 2014 by Johnnie W. Lewis

For information regarding permission, write to:
Franklin Wright Enterprises
1860 Sandy Plains Rd.
Suite 204-150
Marietta, Georgia 30066
info@acloudproductions.com / www.acloudproductions.com

Text copyright © 2014 by Johnnie Wright Lewis
Illustrations copyright © 2013-2014 by Johnnie Wright Lewis
Cover art and design by Johnnie Wright Lewis
Published by Franklin Wright Enterprises.

Printed in U.S.A

Suggestions for Teachers/Parents

1. This book is designed to be READ by a teacher or parent to children or students ages 3-11, to allow for questions and answers. Some children, about 8 or older, can handle the verbiage, but children 12 and older should be advanced enough to read and understand everything in this book, including the "Teacher/Parent Notes" in the back of the book. **Media Specialists:** when checking out this book to Middle School students, point out the supplemental reading in the "Teacher/Parent Notes" section, for enrichment of the text. This book is the second in a series called the *Flutterbye, the Butterfly* series.

2. The section called "Teacher/Parent Notes" in the back of this book is designed to help augment the text of this book. The notes are divided by page applicability, e.g., notes at "Enrichment for page 1," should be read by you, the teacher/parent, before reading the text on page 1, and the information dispensed as you deem appropriate, based on the ages of your audience.

3. Almost all children love to be read to, and shown the pictures from that reading, though not all have the same ability to sit still long enough for the reading of this entire book. Attention spans of children differ, (1)depending on their ages, (2)the time of day/evening the book is read, (3)activities that are planned before or after reading time, and (4)the time of school year that the book is read (is it daylight or dark outside?). Suggested length of reading times include added discussion time to allow for questions and enrichment.
    a. Ages 3-7 -- 20 minutes.
    b. Ages 8-11 -- 30 minutes.
    c. Ages 12 and up -- the entire book.

4. Plan enrichment activities around food chains, or prey and predators in the discussion of "life circles." In the case of "Flutterbye," she is a first generation Monarch butterfly, which means she is born in February/March, and will not migrate as her parents did. First Generation Monarchs are born after their parents return from the southwestern U.S., Mexico, or Florida, and after her emergence from the chrysalis, she will live for 4-7 weeks in the same area as her birth. Although the preceding book in this series, *Flutterbye, the Butterfly,* would not be appropriate for Spring or Summer application or "new life" time frame, this book would, since this First Generation Flutterbye is born, lives and dies in the area of her birth. Also included in the book are NUMEROUS animals and birds that live in the Spring "life circle."

5. Plan a series of discussions on toxicity. Touch on subjects such as environmental impact of man-made toxic materials and wastes as opposed to wastes and materials that are toxic to humanity and animals, but are created by Nature. Such as a Monarch Butterfly and its caterpillars.

6. Plan a teaching unit on defense mechanisms of animals and plants, poison and poisonous creatures as opposed to venom and venomous creatures. Show the differences between those plants, insects, and animals that are poisonous to humans and other animals (to eat, to the touch, etc.) as opposed to those that inject poison into a human or another animal by means of a bite or a stinger. Ex.:
   - A Monarch butterfly is poisonous or toxic to most other creatures if eaten, but it won't hurt you if it lands on you. Its *body* is only toxic to you if its body gets inside yours (or an animal's body). Its defense mechanism is in the hope that you learned from eating the LAST Monarch butterfly, and that you won't want to eat this one.
   - A Rattlesnake injects venom, from poison sacs near its mouth, into its victims if it bites the victim, but its body won't hurt your skin if it glides across it. And eating rattlesnake meat won't hurt you because its flesh does not contain poison, just the poison sacs do. Defense: if you were poisoned by the last bite (or hear its rattles!), you will steer clear of the snake this time.
   - Some plants have stinging nettles, which are toxic if embedded in the skin, designed to keep people and other animals away from it. But eating the flesh of that plant won't kill you. Defense: you will walk around the plant the next time you see one!

7. Plan art, science, research, group, or field trip activities around this book, by teaching a unit on flying creatures (birds and insects), and focusing on:
   a. The importance of insects that pollinate plants.
   b. The differences in plants and their usefulness to an area (Hint: Monarchs like to lay their eggs on milkweed plants [so their baby caterpillars will have something to eat immediately after hatching], which is a weed and not wanted in most cultivated or planned landscape areas. Without milkweed plants, will you get Monarchs to lay eggs?).
   c. Fragility of insects versus their strengths.
   d. Usefulness of flying insects versus crawling insects (and arachnids) versus burrowing insects (and arachnids).
   e. The beauty and symmetry of butterflies' and birds' and dragonflies' wings in flight.
   f. Differences in the ways various butterflies and birds use their wings in flight and at rest. (Hint: most butterflies flap their wings slowly or hold them up together while they rest or eat, whereas most Monarchs leave their wings spread open when they rest, for maximum absorption of the sun).
   g. Draw, color, and cut-out butterflies and birds and hang them from a mobile or from various places around the room, for continual viewing. This will provoke questions and discussions during the day.
   h. A series of essays, for older students, discussing flying creatures and their evolution, psychology, imagery, etc. See the author's books called *The Five Finger Paragraph* series on Amazon.com, for more information on implementation of this suggestion.

DEDICATION

This book, and all such books by me, are dedicated to the child in all of us, who love nature, who love life, and who love butterflies.

Special thanks go to:

★My Better Half, Jimmy Lewis, for his undying love, support, kindness and a second pair of hands!

★My children, Tash Lewis White and Trevor MacKenzie Lewis. I would never have been inspired to write for children if I had not had you. Thanks for your tolerance of your errant mother!

★My "children-in-law," Troy White and Emily Xander Lewis. Though you were not born to me, I love as though you were my own children. Thanks for putting up with me!

★My grandchildren, Parker and Avery White. You are the lights in Mammy's eyes. Thanks for being my audience and sounding boards. I love you!

★All of my "photographers," especially John Humphreys, Jerry Battle, and Sandi Spires Nobles. Your work is impeccable!

★Children everywhere who want to learn about nature in our lives. Chase your dreams as you do butterflies, birds, and bees!

INTRODUCTION

There are four generations of Monarch Butterflies in North America every year. Three generations of Monarchs live and die in the areas of their births, but the fourth generation of Monarchs each year fly to more southern climates, to survive the winter, then return to their home areas to lay eggs before dying.

The "Flutterbye, the Butterfly" you will meet in this book is a First Generation Monarch butterfly, born in February or March of the year. She is a daughter of the Fourth Generation Monarch Butterfly from the first book in this series, by that name. *THAT* Flutterbye lived for six months, flew to Mexico to survive the winter, then came back, and laid her eggs before she died.

THIS Flutterbye will only live for four to eight weeks after she emerges from her chrysalis, living and dying in a small area, of usually two to three acres or less. She will eat (or be eaten!) in the same area where she was born. Her children (Second Generation Monarchs) and her grandchildren (Third Generation Monarchs) will do the same, live in that same area. But her GREAT-grandchildren will be like her mother, Fourth Generation butterflies. And THEY will fly away to the South and come back before they die to lay their eggs.

Flutterbye's friends, the creatures in her **habitat***, are mostly flyers. Like her, they fly from place to place, gathering food. But in those flights, they sometimes become the **prey*** for other creatures, some **terrestrial*** (land-bound), some **arboreal*** (flying). (NOTE: words in **bold** with an asterisk * are defined in the Glossary.)

And now, for the sights and experiences of Flutterbye's life, during the Spring of the year!

Life is a circle. That's one of the "**Laws of Nature***."

Almost all life starts as a "seed" or "egg" of one type or another, which "blooms" or breaks out of its shell, then grows into whatever type of plant or animal that it is supposed to become. Before they die, most of these creatures leave another "seed" or "egg" that will become the next generation. Seed, to plant, to seed. That's a circle. Egg, to grown creature, that produces an egg. That's a **circle of life***.

But many of those circles overlap with the life circles of *other* life circles. Some eggs or seeds become the food for another plant or creature, helping *that* plant or animal to live, grow, and eventually produce a seed or egg of its own.

This is a Monarch Caterpillar egg on a leaf. This is how Flutterbye, the Butterfly started her life!

And this is what Flutterbye looked like when she was a caterpillar.

So. Since it is Spring and there is new life beginning all around her, Flutterbye is going to check out many of the "life circles" in her world, especially the other creatures that are like her, the ones that FLY!

Some of the creatures that live in Flutterbye's little area live on or under the ground. Others swim or live above the ground, flying from one area to another to gather or eat their food. Some animals and flyers eat seeds and plants and grasses. Some eat other smaller animals like frogs, fish, snakes, and snails. Some flyers, like Flutterbye, never *eat* anything — they drink their food! Some flyers must worry about being EATEN by other birds and animals. And some flyers are the ones EATING other birds and animals!

Spring time CAN be a beautiful time. The flowers are blooming, the air is getting warmer after a cold winter, tiny animals and birds and insects are being born, those tiny animals and birds and insects that were just born are hungry, mother and father birds are feeding their babies with insects and… WAIT!! That means…, that if one animal is to *grow,* by eating insects and small animals, those insects and small animals have to… DIE! ARGH!!

Unfortunately, THAT'S another one of the **laws of Nature***. Too many mosquitoes are hatched because *some* of them will become the food of larger birds and animals, yet still leave a few mosquitoes to live and produce more eggs for the next batch of animals that need to be fed. A circle. **Eat or be eaten**, that's a (first?) **law of Nature***.

*Baby Blue Jays are **born** begging for food.*

*And here's a young Mayfly that does **not** want to BECOME the baby Blue Jays' food!*

3

Even Flutterbye and her brothers and sisters could become food for some **animals∞**, if they are not careful! Monarch butterflies, like Flutterbye, drink nothing but nectar. But when they were caterpillars, they needed to eat LOTS of milkweed in order to grow. In fact, each Monarch caterpillar can eat every leaf and most stems on two or more milkweed plants — *per day!!* **(∞See ENRICHMENT NOTE on page 29 about Monarchs' toxicity).**

But, after their chrysalis state, when they change from caterpillars to butterflies, all butterflies, including Monarchs, *never eat their food again!* They simply sip nectar from flowers, through a **proboscis***, all day, every day.

4

Almost every kind of animal, bird, and insect falls into one of two categories —
prey* or **predator***. It's hard to think about a bird or chipmunk or even a dragonfly
or butterfly being EATEN by something, but remember the First Law of Nature? Eat
or be Eaten. And some of these creatures fall into BOTH categories. They can eat
other smaller animals and then become the food for a larger animal. So the best
we can do is enjoy watching the creatures around us while they are here.

Caterpillars, bees, butterflies, dragonflies, flies, and most other insects are on lots
of different animals' "menus." If a lizard is going to eat a worm or caterpillar, then
that lizard might become dinner for the next Great Blue Heron that comes along!

"Army worms"   *Blue Lizard*

Great Blue Heron

Most of Flutterbye's flying friends are at the bottom of the **food chain***. That means, there's always "something bigger" that's trying to eat them. But most of the insects on that bottom level have other purposes in life, too — to spread pollen from one plant to another while they are trying to get their nectar and to spread JOY to people, just by looking COOL and flying around! Yes, in their **larva*** stages (that is the caterpillar stage, in butterflies) they eat, and sometimes destroy, plants. But, by eating only milkweed plants (poisonous to most other animals), Monarch caterpillars are actually SAVING other animals, by eating the milkweed themselves!

Most insects become the food of some other creature, whether it's a two-legged, four-legged, or six-legged creature.

Ooohh! That sounds like a MATH problem. If a six-legged creature, say a dragonfly, eats another six-legged creature, say a housefly, how many legs went to dinner at the "**Prey to Go**" restaurant? Then, how many legs came out ALIVE?!?

Obviously, not all insects are eaten by something bigger. It's just that there are TOO MANY of the little boogers around for them to ALL be eaten! Here are some more, in addition to the ones on the previous page, of the items on the menu at that "**Prey to Go**" restaurant. Some of these insects, like the Praying Mantis and the dragonflies, are also predators!

Grasshopper

Widow Skimmer Dragonfly

Ladybug

Potato Beetle

Blue Dragonfly

Caterpillar

Garden Snail

Bumble Bee

Green Sweat Bee

Praying Mantis

Prey* or **predator*, predator*** or **prey*,** which would you rather be? Eat or be eaten? Here are some more flying creatures that might look like dinner to a **predator*.** There are FOUR insects here that are teensy tiny, about the size of a pencil point. Which ones do you think they are? The answers are on page 30.

Blue Darter Dragonfly

Honeybees

Aedes Mosquito

Bumblebee

Mealy Bugs

Aphids

Stink Bug

Tarnished Weevil

Boll Weevil

Silverleaf Whitefly

Golden-back Beetle

Pirate Bug and Silver Whitefly Nymphs

8

You would not think that small insects would eat insects, would you? Well, they have to eat SOMETHING to stay alive! Anything that is its own size or smaller is fair game for dragonflies!! Dragonflies, and their smaller cousins the damselflies, live all over the world in a RAINBOW of colors from red and orange to yellow, blue, green, and black.

They live mostly in swampy or watery areas where they lay their eggs, usually, under the water or in mud. Sometimes, their babies, called **naiads***, live underwater near where they hatched, eating mosquito larvae and other smaller water bugs (that were hatched in the same water), for longer than you may have been alive! TRUE! Some dragonflies' **naiads*** will live underwater for up to ten years, before they decide to climb out of their oozy homes, climb to the top of a reed or branch in the water, and hang on to dry out. When the skin in completely dried out, it will break open and out crawls a fully grown dragonfly, ready to eat or be eaten!

There are a few differences between dragonflies and damselflies. See if you can see the differences (below and on the next page.). Dragonflies have both eyes on the front of its head, their front and back wings are different shapes, and they rest with their wings straight out to the sides, perpendicular to their bodies (but they *might* rest with their wings pointing a little toward their heads).

Dragonflies

Eyes in front, born to hunt…

Damselflies are usually smaller than dragonflies, have one eye on each side of their heads, their front and back wings are the same shape, and they rest with their wings parallel to their bodies.

Do you think that old **adage***, "eyes in front, born to hunt, eyes on side, born to hide" is true for dragonflies and damselflies?

Damselfly eating a fly!

...eyes on side, born to hide!

The bees are another type of "flyers" in Flutterbye's world. All species of bees serve at least one purpose in common — to help pollinate plants. Sure, honeybees make honey, which is an important food for humans and other animals. But, transferring pollen is important, too. Pollen needs to be transferred from one plant to another. Transferred pollen helps those plants create fruit and nectar for animals, and for people to eat and enjoy. And bees help do that transferring!

So, *while* those honeybees and hornets and wasps and dirt daubers are busy trying to get their nectar from flowers, they are also playing "postal carrier" for something else. They're carrying pollen to other flowers!

But have you ever thought about how those tiny little creatures pick up and carry the pollen from one plant to another? They don't have big enough hands to carry the tiny little yellow grains of pollen, so they carry it — on their bodies! See those hairs on the bee's back? Watch what he can DO with those hairs!

11

As the bumblebee burrows deeper down into the flower, trying to drink the nectar down deep inside the flower, it keeps bumping into the stamen stems, knocking the pollen off and onto the bee. See how the bee gets more pollen on its body, as it digs deeper into the flower to get to the nectar? And when it finally finishes drinking all the nectar, it flies to the next flower. Some of that pollen on its body falls off as it wiggles around in the new flower. Now, the new flower will be pollinated!

As they drink nectar from flowers, Flutterbye and her friends get a little pollen on them, too, like her friend the yellow swallowtail here. But the swallowtail does not get NEARLY as much pollen on her body as the bee does, because she can sit on the edge of the flower and stick her long **proboscis*** down into the flower to drink up the sweet stuff!

Yellow Swallowtail Butterfly

Red-Throated Hummingbirds

Emerald Hummingbird

Did you know that there is a bird that can fly BACKWARD? Hummingbirds can! And they are the *only* **species*** of bird that can fly forward, backward, up, down and stay still *while in the air!* In the dining room department, hummingbirds are almost **omnivorous*,** which means that they can eat more than one variety of food. They drink nectar in flowers or feeders you put out for them, plus some "other things." And, they do have **gizzards***, even though they don't eat seeds. The **gizzard*** helps to break up the other things that they eat, since they do not have **gall bladders*** to help break up those things. Those "other things" that they eat, that need the gizzard's help, are tiny little **arthropods*** (insects), especially when they are about to start their annual migrations to the north (in the Spring) or south (in the Autumn). Those birds have to be able to fly for 18 to 24 hours straight, without stopping, if they are one of the varieties that flies back over the Gulf of Mexico toward warmer weather in the north.

There are about 250 species of hummingbirds in the Americas (both North and South America). Some are tiny (the Bee Hummingbird is about 1 1/2 inches long!) and some are huge, for a hummingbird (up to 5 inches!). The Ruby Throated Hummingbird is the one most often seen in North America.

Want to know how fast their tiny wings flap? Let's pretend you are a hummingbird, but you are going to use your tongue to represent the speed of their wings. Blow air over your tipped-up tongue, so that it goes "duh-duh-duh-duh-duh" in your mouth. Faster!! Think you're flapping your wings fast enough? Wrong! A hummer's wings flap MUCH, MUCH, faster, like between 70 to 120 beats PER SECOND! That's right, per *SECOND.* You would NOT make a very convincing hummingbird! And if you wanted to take a picture of the hummer while it's flying, you would have to have a very good camera to catch those wings, so they do **NOT** look blurred!

Flutterbye has learned, during the weeks since she hatched from her **chrysalis***, that most birds and other flying creatures eat seeds and plants as their food *ALONG WITH* insects and small animals. Of course, Flutterbye tries to AVOID anything that's bigger than her, anything that might want to eat her! But, it is usually the small birds that eat seeds, plants, and smaller insects (though not always!) and the larger ones that eat larger plants, larger insects and animals (though not always!). If a bird or animal eats seeds, insects, and other animals, it is said to be **omnivorous***.

What does this blue bird see in the water in the bird bath?

Every evening, MILLIONS of bats fly out of Carlsbad Caverns in New Mexico to feed on gazillions of mosquitoes and other flying insects, like Flutterbye's cousins, the moths. Moths usually fly at night, though butterflies usually fly in the daytime.

Bats are not birds, even though they fly. They are mammals, like you! They feed milk to their babies, they have furry hair instead of feathers, and teeth and tongues, along with rather poor eyesight. Instead of using their eyes to find their food, they use **echolocation,*** by sending out high-pitched "sound waves" that bounce off objects and back. These "sound signals" tell them where they are so they don't bump into things. It also tells them where the insects are so they can get ready for dinner! Bats sleep during the day, in dark places, and come out at night to eat those night-flying insects. If Flutterbye is flying at night, will she be safe from bats?

Every night, a single bat can eat an average of 800 mosquitoes an hour or huge numbers of moths, beetles, and other flying insects. Helps keep the insect population in check!

The same types of insects, along with butterflies and moths, are chased during the day by small reptiles and amphibians. Snakes even eat frogs and lizards and other snakes! Talk about *omnivorous*!*

Most medium- and small-sized birds eat seeds and small insects, and yes, some of them might try to eat Flutterbye, when they are not eating seeds! Flutterbye is REALLY afraid of the the much LARGER flying creatures AND land animals that will eat just about *anything!*

Nuthatch

Mourning Dove

Northern Flicker

Female and Male Cardinals

Baltimore Oriole

Northern Mockingbird

Seagulls

Sparrows and Finches

More seed and insect eaters are found almost everywhere.

Rooster and Hen

Quail (Bob White)

American Robin

Red-headed
Woodpecker

Chipping Sparrow

Red-bellied
Woodpecker

Golden Finch

Baby birds, but can you guess
what kind? See page 32.

These lizards, frogs, and a snake, and even small mammals, will eat small flying creatures (remember the bats?), along with anything else they can capture, like birds, butterflies, and other insects.

Zebra-tailed Lizard

Leaf Green Tree Frog

Corn Snake
(non-venomous*)

Green Anole

Male
Green
Frog

Bearded Iguana

Desert Spiny
Lizard

Gerbil

Because alligators and snakes do not have bacon and eggs on a plate or a bowl of cereal for breakfast, they have to go after their own versions of breakfast. Bigger animals do not eat as many insects as they do smaller animals and birds. And a hungry snake *probably* would not by-pass a tasty butterfly, if he has not been able to find a fat rat to eat! These larger reptiles and water animals usually eat small- to medium-sized birds, along with eating some of the smaller reptiles on the previous page (and maybe a few insects). Bigger animals have bigger appetites, so just eating a little Flutterbye wouldn't help them much, would it?

American Alligator

Carp

Ball Python

Brown Snake

Green Snake

Russian Tortoise

20

And even though it may seem like **cannibalism*** for larger birds to eat smaller birds and other flying creatures, it does happen. There's a certain hawk that continually keeps the rat population down in the author's backyard, but has to be scared away when it sees the small birds, chipmunks, and squirrels feasting around the bird feeders! Big birds will eat almost anything that does not try to eat them first!

Nesting Ospreys

Albino Peahen and Guinea Pig

White Egret

Peacock

Trumpeter Swan and her Goslings

Crowned Crane

Great Blue Heron

Osprey with fish

Great Gray Owl

Emu

22

Great Blue Heron

Osprey

Wood Cranes

Brown Pelican

Sandhill Cranes

This is one that you will probably *never* see in person. An albatross, a sea bird that is as big as a turkey, is sitting in the water, when a great white shark decides he wants to see how the bird tastes!

And here's another one you may never see again. What goes *into* the bird, must come out. Somehow!

So. NOW we know why Flutterbye is so cautious around other creatures, including birds and other animals, and even humans.

Flutterbye can not eat anything except nectar. But she can be EATEN by almost anything else that crawls, flies, or swims! And her caterpillars, when they hatch, might be eaten by any of those same creatures that crawls, flies, or swims!

Flying birds and animals sip nectar, eat insects, and each other, including other smaller insects, birds, reptiles, and mammals.

Let's see. We have talked about a few of the "**laws of Nature***." The first and most important is "eat or be eaten." After that, remember the "circle of life"? Seed to plant to seed? That's a second **Law of Nature***. Produce young animals or seeds for the next generation.

We talked about the "**life circle***," in which a plant or animal starts as a seed or egg, grows up, then has a seed or egg of its own. That's just like Flutterbye, whose circle of life was from an egg on a leaf, to a caterpillar, to a butterfly, to an egg on a leaf.

When Flutterbye lays her eggs, the caterpillars that hatch from those eggs will become the second generation Monarch butterflies. .They will live from April or May to June or July. Read more about the next generation of Monarch butterflies in *Flutterbye Flits, Floats, and Flies.*

Now, aren't you glad we had this little talk today? Admit it, it was fun, wasn't it?!?

***Chrysalis of a Monarch Butterfly…,
like Flutterbye!***

25

GLOSSARY

adage -- *noun* \ˈa-dij\ an old and well-known saying that expresses a general truth.

arboreal -- *adjective* \är-ˈbȯr-ē-əl\ (1)of or relating to trees; (2)living in or found in trees.

arthropods -- *noun* \ˈär-thrə-ˌpäd\ any of a phylum or group (Arthropoda) of invertebrate animals (those without an internal skeleton, such as insects, arachnids, and crustaceans) that have a segmented body and jointed appendages, a usually chitinous exoskeleton molted at intervals, and a dorsal anterior brain connected to a ventral chain of ganglia. Ants, roaches, beetles, butterflies, mosquitoes, etc.

cannibalism -- *noun* \ˈka-nə-bə-ˌli-zəm\ (1)the usually ritualistic eating of human flesh by a human being; (2) the eating of the flesh of an animal by another animal of the same kind.

chrysalis -- *noun* \ˈkri-sə-ləs\: (1)a moth or butterfly at the stage of growth when it is turning into an adult and is enclosed in a hard case; (2) a hard case that protects a moth or butterfly while it is turning into an adult.

circle of life -- noun/ biology: the series of stages through which a living thing passes from the beginning of its life until its death.

echolocation -- *noun* \ek-o-lo-ka'-shən\: a process for locating distant or invisible objects by means of sound waves reflected from the objects back to the sender.

food chain -- *noun*\ a series of organisms in which each uses the next member, usually lower on the chain, of the series as a food source. Example: lions eat gazelles, gazelles eat ants, ants eat aphids.

gall bladder -- *noun*\\ˈgȯl-ˌbla-dər\ *medical* : the organ in the body in which bile from the liver is stored; helps the body break down particles of food.

gizzard -- *noun* \ˈgi-zərd\ a part in the stomach of a bird or insect in which food is broken down into small pieces.

habitat -- *noun* \ˈha-bə-ˌtat\ the place or type of place where a plant or animal naturally or normally lives or grows. Example: where a bear normally roams, his "neighborhood."

larva -- *noun* \ˈlär-və\pl. larvae\ a very young form of an insect that often looks like a worm.

laws of Nature -- *noun*\ a group of rules or specific principles held to be derived from Nature and binding upon human society in the absence of or in addition to positive law.

naiads -- *noun* \ˈnā-əd, ˈnī-, -ˌad\ plural na·iads or na·ia·des\ (1)an aquatic larval form of an animal or insect; (2)an insect nymph (as of a mayfly, dragonfly, damselfly, or stone fly).

non-venomous -- *adjective* \ non-ˈve-nə-məs\ (1)NOT capable of putting poison or venom into another animal's body by biting or stinging it; (2) containing NO venom.

omnivorous -- *adjective* \äm-ˈniv-rəs, -ˈni-və-\ (1)eating both plants and animals; (2)eager to learn about many different things.

predator -- *noun* \ˈpre-də-tər, -ˌtȯr\ (1)an animal that lives by killing and eating other animals; (2)an animal that preys on other animals; (3)a person who looks for other people in order to use, control, or harm them in some way.

prey -- *noun* \ˈprā\ (1)an animal that is hunted or killed by another animal for food; (2)someone who is easily harmed or affected in a bad way by someone or something.

proboscis -- noun \prə-ˈbä-səs, -ˈbäs-kəs\ biology: (1)the long, thin nose of some animals (such as an elephant); (2)a long, thin tube that forms part of the mouth of some insects (such as a butterfly); (3)a person's nose, especially when it is very long or big.

species -- *noun* \ˈspē-(ˌ)shēz, -(ˌ)sēz\ *biology*: (1)a group of animals or plants that are similar and can produce young animals or plants; (2)a group (that is smaller than a genus) of related animals or plants;(3) a particular group of things or people that belong together or have some shared quality.

terrestrial - - *adjective* \tə-ˈres-t(r)ē-əl\(1)relating to or occurring on the earth; (2)living or growing on land instead of in water or air.

venomous -- *adjective* \ˈve-nə-məs\ (1)capable of putting poison or venom into another animal's body usually by biting or stinging it; (2)containing venom sacs.

27

TEACHER/PARENT NOTES
(only those pages requiring "enrichment" or "enhancement" will have Enrichment NOTES)

Enrichment for pages 1-2

Here are illustrations to represent a "circle of life," or "life circle." One for a plant, one for a butterfly, and one for a frog. Enlarge these drawings and show students the points at which the three circles might overlap. Or use the drawings as an augmentation of a discussion on the "food chain," asking the question, "If the Butterfly feeds on the flower, and the Frog feeds on the Caterpillar (or the Butterfly), what might feed on the frog?"

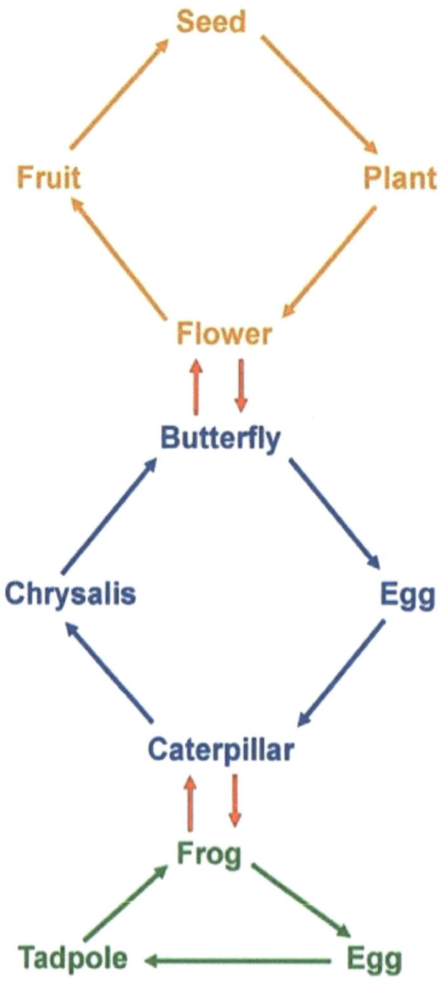

Seed

Fruit   Plant

Flower

Butterfly

Chrysalis   Egg

Caterpillar

Frog

Tadpole ⟵ Egg

Typical Food Chain

Alligator
(top of chain)

Crane

Snake

Frog

Dragonfly

Housefly

Gnat

Aphid
(bottom of chain)

Enrichment for page 3

Consider introducing the idea of a list of the "laws of Nature." "Laws of Nature" per se, are subjective "ideas" that are not always agreed upon. What is or should be a "law" to one person may be a "non-issue" to another. As there are no hard and fast rules as to which "laws" would be on the list, this is good time to begin a discussion on hard and fast FACTS (objective, concrete, tangible "things" that they can touch and feel and observe with their five senses) versus the nebulous concepts of IDEAS (subjective, abstract, based on opinions; not observable with the five senses, but come from "things" that are thought of and compiled rather than observed).

========================

Enrichment for page 4

Good time for a lesson on toxicity, including what constitutes toxic versus safe for consumption and use. And instinct. And conservation. Monarch butterflies lay their eggs exclusively on milkweed plants (or near them, if they can find them). Milkweed plants are toxic to most other creatures, but the Monarch caterpillars devour the leaves and stems from the moment that they hatch, eating or looking for more plants continuously, up to the time they molt their last skins, which become their chrysalises. Consumption of the milkweed leaves makes their bodies toxic to other creatures that eat them, either killing them or making them very sick. Through instinct and observation of other creatures of their kind, most creatures have learned NOT to eat the highly colorfully striped Monarch caterpillars and equally as colorful, and toxic, butterflies.

========================

Enrichment for page 5

The Animal Kingdom is made of those that prey on others and those that ARE the prey of others. Prey and Predators. Have students make lists of animals, insects and plants that they believe to be the prey of others. Then make lists of those animals, insects, and plants that they believe to be the predators of others. Now compare the lists to see common names on both lists. Bring this discussion around to previous discussions on the "circle of life" and on Food Chains. Have students draw food chains that include plants or animals on both of their lists.

==========================

Enrichment for page 6

Extend the "Enrichment for page 4" by discussing adaptations that various animals and plants have made that contribute to the continuation of the food chain. Monarch caterpillars have evolved to the point that the substance in milkweed plants that poisons other plants and animals does not bother them. But it makes their flesh poisonous to others, making them uneatable by other animals (and possibly,

Enrichment for page 6 (cont.)
making them the "bottom of that food chain").

Form student research groups to see if animals can be found that could eat Monarch caterpillars or butterflies, yet not be harmed. Perhaps a competition between groups planned around a field trip to a butterfly garden in the school yard or elsewhere.
========================

Enrichment for page 7
Discuss the parts of insects' bodies (thorax, abdomen, etc.) and compare the differences with the human body. Number of segments, which segments have the legs, or the antennae, or the other "appendages" on the creature.

Discuss the parts of arachnids bodies, as opposed to insects' bodies. Point out the differences between insects and arachnids, as well as the similarities.
========================

Enrichment for page 8
Answers to the question on page 8 are: Mealy Bugs, Aphids, Silverleaf Whiteflies, and Silverleaf Whitefly Nymphs. Aphids and Mealy Bugs appear as little white dots that move on the underside of a leaf, where they hide from their predators. The Pirate Bug that feeds on the Nymphs doesn't qualify as pencil-point size, since he is as large as 1/4" long.
========================

Enrichment for page 9
Discuss symbiotic relationships and ecosystems, with the various residents and members of the separate systems related to or dependent on the others in the system for their livelihood, food, grooming, protection, etc. Have students make lists of examples as they wander around the school yard or on a field trip.
========================

Enrichment for page 10
Make a game out of the old adage, "Eyes in front, born to hunt, Eyes on side, born to hide." Divide the class into groups, each with two lists to write on. As animals' pictures are flashed on a screen, students quickly write down whether or not that animal would NORMALLY be the prey or predator. Have one student in each group read his/her group's list to the class. Group with the most correct answers, wins. Now pick a prize for that group, such as getting to line up first to go on the next field trip to count butterflies in the butterfly garden.
========================

Enrichment for page 11, 12, and 13
Discuss pollen and pollination of plants and flowers, allowing students to label or draw and label pictures of the cross-sections of flower parts. For younger students, that may be the end of the discussion, discussing the ways that bees and flying insects help with the pollination of plants. For older students (fifth grades and up), this could be the beginning of discussions on reproduction.

This is also the time to discuss possible ecological ramifications to numerous bee populations dying off without explanation. Or the time to discuss the Africanization of American bee populations.
===========================

Enrichment for page 14
North American hummingbirds migrate much further south than do Monarch butterflies. In fact, as far south as Panama, Colombia, and Venezuela. That means that some hummingbirds brave flying over the Gulf of Mexico. But, actually only in one direction. Flying south, MOST hummingbirds follow the coast of the Gulf, apparently to avoid the Gulf during hurricane season.

But flying north, several varieties of hummingbirds fatten up on insects in Central and South America for a few weeks before tackling the arduous 18-24 hour trip across the Gulf of Mexico with no planned stops. They have been known to land on ships passing through the area, but since that's not a given point, they only land if they sight the ship. Otherwise, they fly straight through, sometimes landing in Cuba for a while, then following the warming weather northward toward Florida and other southern states around the Gulf. Males leave their winter grounds about 10 days ahead of females. Most hummingbirds live 2-5 years, but some species live up to 10 years.
===========================

Enrichment for page 15
Butterfly instinct demands that the flyers steer clear of anything bigger than they are or that they sense might be a threat to them. This does not explain why some butterflies will come up to much, MUCH larger animals and rest on them — on humans, cows, deer, etc. Is this because they sense that we won't hurt them, but that something smaller than humans, say a cat or tortoise, might want to taste them? Nice question to ponder with children.
=====================

Enrichment for page 16
Bats are carnivorous mammals that give live birth to their young, feed them on milk from mammary glands, and protect them from harm. Like most mammals. They also teach their young to feed on

Enrichment for page 16 (cont.)
insects at night, after they're big enough to fly, in 2-5 weeks.

About 45 species of bats live in the USA and few of them migrate to the warmer climates, but those that do, only go as far south as southern Mexico. Some of those that do migrate south for the winter return to the same caves that they lived in previously. Some hibernate, rather than migrate, while others live in hollow trees year around.

There are MANY myths about bats that have scared people for hundreds of years. One is that they suck animal blood. Only the vampire bat drinks blood and it does not suck it. It cuts a tiny slit, with its sharp teeth, in the sleeping cow or deer's neck, producing a liquid anesthesia so the process doesn't hurt the animal, and drinks the blood as it flows — about 2 tablespoons worth. Not enough to kill or harm the animal. Another myth is that bats will get caught in ones hair. A bat's echolocation is so precise that it can avoid an object as thin as a piece of thread. Why would it fly into your hair if it could avoid it? Another myth is that all bats carry rabies. Less than 1% do carry rabies, which is less than in the normal dog, cat, and fox populations.

MANY movies, books, songs, and other pieces of entertainment have been made and written over the years, extolling the "fear" of bats as blood-sucking, evil creatures, but most of this "hype" is just that. Fiction designed to sell the created work with a "scary" theme. Very little truth lies in any of the works.

A single bat can eat up to 1000 mosquitoes in one night, making it very beneficial to an area in controlling the insect populations. So much for fiction.
=============================

Enrichment for page 17 and 18
Most birds are omnivorous, meaning that they eat seeds and insects. And most of the larger birds eat more than that. Most wading bird (herons, egrets, cranes) eat small animals they find on land or water. However, there is one large bird that only eats seeds, tubers, roots and plant matter it finds in the water — Canadian Geese. Strange, but true. Their cousins, however, the grey or white geese that live on farms, will eat seeds AND insects and small animals. The baby birds on the tank are baby Blue Jays.
=============================

Enrichment for page 19 and 20
Although they are not part of the "flying friends" on which this book focuses, small reptiles and small mammals are an important part of the ecosystem of the larger flying birds.

32

Enrichment for page 19 and 20 (cont.)
Frogs, lizards, iguanas, geckos, and snakes, along with rats, mice, gerbils, and guinea pigs (and other small mammals) will eat any smaller animals they can find. This literally puts them in the middle of the food chains between flying insects, flying birds and animals. Insects and small birds are eaten by the small reptiles and small mammals mentioned, which in turn, are eaten by larger birds and reptiles.
==============================

Enrichment for page 21, 22, and 23
Large carnivorous birds, such as eagles, hawks, osprey, falcons, and other birds with hooked beaks, eat only small animals, like squirrels, rats, chipmunks, etc. (they don't eat seeds and plants). And since small birds can't fly as rapidly as those large birds do, they also fall prey to the predator birds. Rarely do the large water birds, such as herons, cranes, egrets, etc., eat small birds (they usually eat fish, frogs, snails, etc. in the water), but if they were starving, who can say?

The question is, since they are both birds, if an eagle eats a sparrow, is that considered cannibalism? It's doubtful that birds have the level of consciousness to worry about such matters!
==============================

Enrichment for page 24
As water birds are usually at the top of their food chain, it is hard to imagine them as the prey for anything. But large bird carcasses line the edges of rivers and swamps where herons, cranes, egrets, albatrosses, storks, etc. and other carnivores, such as alligators, large constrictor snakes (like boas and pythons) come in contact with each other. A crane standing in the shallows of the Everglades must look like a tempting treat to an underwater alligator.

P.S. That picture of the Osprey "letting go" is NOT doctored!! One of the author's friends caught that as it was happening!! That's a "One in a Million" shot, John Humphreys!
==============================

Enrichment for page 26
The End.

33

Acknowledgements

The following people were kind enough to submit their own photographs for this book. Photographs in the public domain are so noted. All illustrations are by Johnnie W. Lewis.

Jerry Battle: pages 3 (baby birds, right), 5 (army worms, heron), 6 (orange and yellow BF in center, big-footed fly, widow skimmer dragonfly), 14 (center left, bottom center), 17 (mockingbird, northern flicker), 18 (American Robin), 20 (brown snake), 22 (great blue heron), 23 (great blue heron)

Rhonda Edge Brock: page 3 (baby birds, left)

Libby Butgereit: page 20 (ball python, named "Dex")

Brooke Rowland Erwin: page 18 (Golden Finch)

Allison Howard: pages 2 (deer), 7 (caterpillar, bumble bee), 9 (upper left), 17 (Baltimore Oriole), 18 (baby birds), 19 (Leaf Green Tree Frogs, green anole, gerbil)

Johnnie W. Lewis: pages 1, 2 (tortoise, dolphin), 4 (center), 8 (stinkbug), 17 (mourning dove, seagulls), 18 (chipping sparrow), 22 (emu)

Suzan Hughes-Kennedy: pages 2 (lizard), 7 (praying mantis)

John Humphreys: pages 3 (baby birds, center), 5 (blue lizard), 6 (upper left BF, hornet, black and white butterfly, bottom right BF, housefly), 7 (blue dragonfly), 11, 12, 13, 17 (nuthatch), 18 (red-bellied and red-headed woodpeckers), 19 (corn snake, bearded iguana), 20 (American alligator, Russian tortoise), 21 (nesting ospreys, egret), 22 (osprey with fish), 23 (brown pelican, wood cranes, osprey), 24 (osprey)

Julia Sallee Ligosh: page 14 (lower right)

Donna Lique Mock: page 8 (Blue Darter Dragonfly)

Sandi's (Spires Nobles) Photography: pages 2 (caterpillar), 3 (mayfly), 4 (4 Monarch photos), 6 (upper right, ladybugs, orange butterfly on second row), 7 (ladybug), 8 (bumble bee), 9 (upper right, lower left and right), 14 (upper right, center), 15, 17 (female and male cardinals, sparrows and finches, 19 (Yellow Tree Frog, Male Green frog)

Sharon Woodard Oliver: page 21 (peacock)

Mandy Schreiner: page 2 (gecko), 6 (green and black butterfly)

Alissa Wright Wilkerson: page 2 (horses)

Public Domain photos from USDA sites: page 7 (grasshopper, potato beetle, garden snail, green sweat bee), 8 (honeybees, Aedes mosquito, mealy bugs, tarnished weevil, silver leaf whitefly and nymphs, boll weevil, aphids, pirate bug, golden-backed beetle), 10, 14 (Emerald Hummingbird),16, 18 (rooster and hen, quail), 19 (zebra-tailed lizard, desert spiny lizard), 20 (carp, green snake), 21 (peahen and guinea pig, Swan and goslings), 22 (crowned crane, great grey owl), 23 (sandhill cranes), 24 (shark and albatross)

34

Even though we are not always kind to our animal friends, we still erect statues in their honor, so we may view them through the ages. Enjoy!

Taken at "Gibbs Gardens" in Marble Hill, GA

Public Domain

Taken from the author's stash of pictures, these are the only ants allowed inside her house!